D1297770

DETERMINED TO WIN

CHILDREN LIVING WITH ALLERGIES AND ASTHMA

DON'T TURN AWAY

For a free color catalog describing Gareth Stevens' list of high-quality books, call 1-800-341-3569 (USA) or 1-800-461-9120 (Canada).

Don't Turn Away
Meeting the Challenge: Children Living with Diabetes
Moments that Disappear: Children Living with Epilepsy
Going Places: Children Living with Cerebral Palsy
Finding a Common Language: Children Living with Deafness
One Day at a Time: Children Living with Leukemia
Seeing in Special Ways: Children Living with Blindness
We Laugh, We Love, We Cry: Children Living with Mental Retardation
On Our Own Terms: Children Living with Physical Disabilities
Determined to Win: Children Living with Allergies and Asthma

ISBN 0-8368-1075-9

North American edition first published in 1994 by

Gareth Stevens Publishing
1555 North RiverCenter Drive, Suite 201
Milwaukee, Wisconsin 53212, USA

Published in Sweden under the title *Isabell en vanlig tjej – med astma och allergi.*

Editors: Amy Bauman and Barbara J. Behm
Series designer: Kate Kriege
Designer: Kristi Ludwig

1 2 3 4 5 6 7 8 9 99 98 97 96 95 94

Printed in the United States of America

DETERMINED TO WIN

CHILDREN LIVING WITH ALLERGIES AND ASTHMA

DON'T TURN AWAY

Thomas Bergman

Gareth Stevens Publishing
MILWAUKEE

A child with allergies is overly sensitive to certain substances entering the body. A child with asthma has a condition that makes breathing difficult. The following photographic story shows six-year-old Isabell — a child dealing with both diseases. It is my hope that in showing how Isabell lives at home, at the day-care center, and at the hospital, people will better understand children like Isabell and be sympathetic toward them. It's important that people take these diseases seriously.

Isabell has been affected by allergies since she was three months old. When she was two, the doctors discovered she had asthma, as well. Now six, Isabell goes to an ordinary day-care center. She thinks about growing older and hopes that, as she does, she will outgrow her allergies. She wants to be able to go to friends' houses the way her classmates do, eat the foods the others eat, and simply do what other children do. She even dreams of one day working with dogs at an animal hospital.

I would like to offer warm thanks to Isabell and her family for letting me photograph her and write about her. I would also like to thank Dr. Gunilla Hedlin of the Allergy Department at the child clinic of Huddinge Hospital, and Åke Hedin, a representative of "Young Allergy Sufferers" (RmA). In Sweden, this group is a national association called "Riksförbundet mot Astma-Allergi" that has helped me with facts, information, and practical questions. Finally, I'd like to thank the children and teachers at the day-care center of Skärlingebacken!

Thomas Bergman

Thomas Bergman

It is with great pride that we bring our readers another title in the Don't Turn Away *series.* Determined to Win *is an inspiring portrait of a special young girl named Isabell. Although her allergies and asthma have affected her physically most of her life, she has not let these conditions get the best of her heart, soul, and spirit.*

Thomas Bergman's remarkable photographs bring Isabell's story to life with stunning clarity. Bergman's heartfelt words serve to teach readers of any age a quality that we need to encourage in modern times — compassion for one another.

Gareth Stevens

Gareth Stevens
Publisher

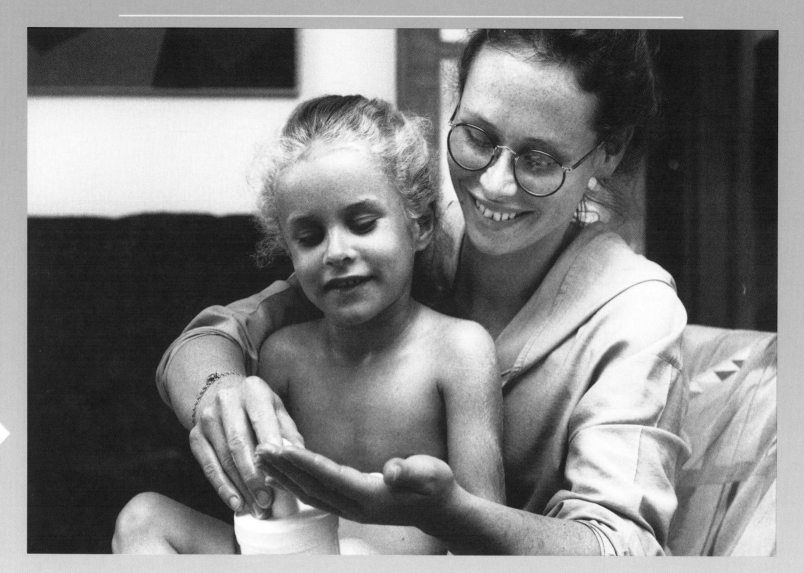

ISABELL

This is Isabell, a six-year-old girl who has both allergies and asthma. She lives with her mother, Lotta, and her big brother, Frederick. From birth, Isabell has had dry skin. At times, it was so dry that it fell off in big hunks from several places on her body. That's when the doctors discovered she had eczema. Before Isabell was one year old, the doctors also found that she was allergic to cow's milk and other foods. She has been on a special diet ever since. From the age of two, Isabell has also struggled with asthma. She takes daily medicines that make it easier for her to breathe. At times, breathing has been so difficult that she has even been taken to the hospital.

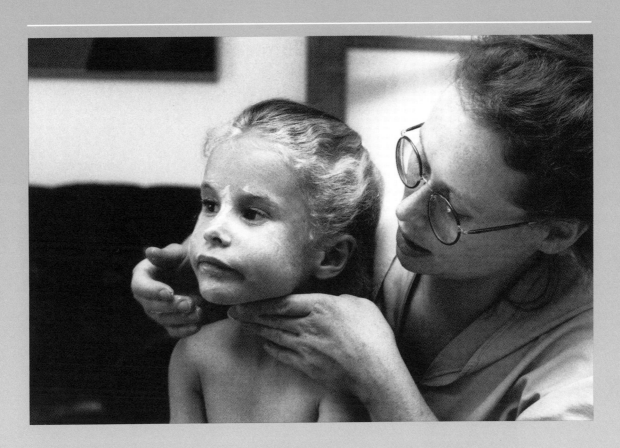

Every weekday, the alarm clock rings at 5:00 A.M. Isabell and her mother
must get up, but Frederick can sleep a while longer. Today, as Isabell comes
to the breakfast table, she is still sleepy. She has not slept well. Her mother
can see this as she hands Isabell a bowl of warm cereal. As Isabell eats, she
talks about everything that she wants to do today. Then she remembers
that she must go to the hospital this morning.

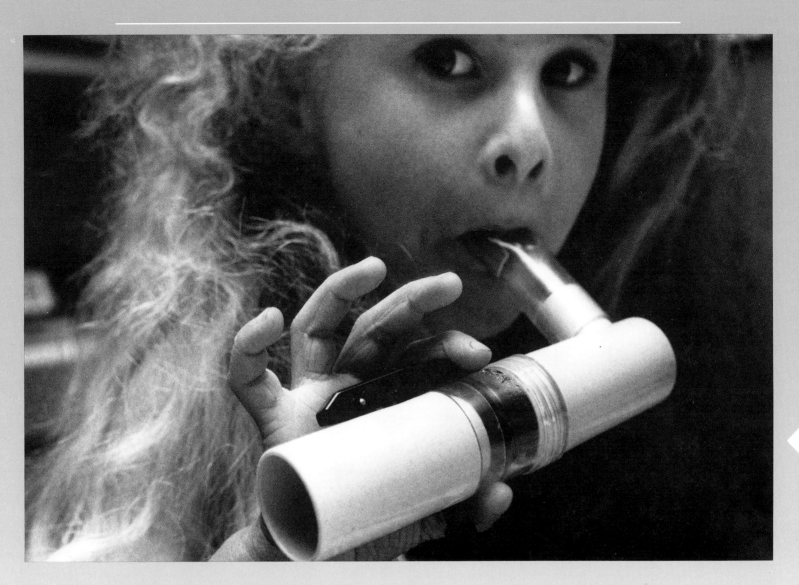

Isabell finishes eating and begins her morning routine. First, she bathes. After that, her mother rubs salves into her skin. The salves are supposed to make Isabell's skin soft and prevent itching and irritation. Next comes the inhaler with medicine that helps Isabell breathe easier. Then, at last, she dresses, and Isabell is ready to go to the hospital. Her mother and Frederick are coming, too.

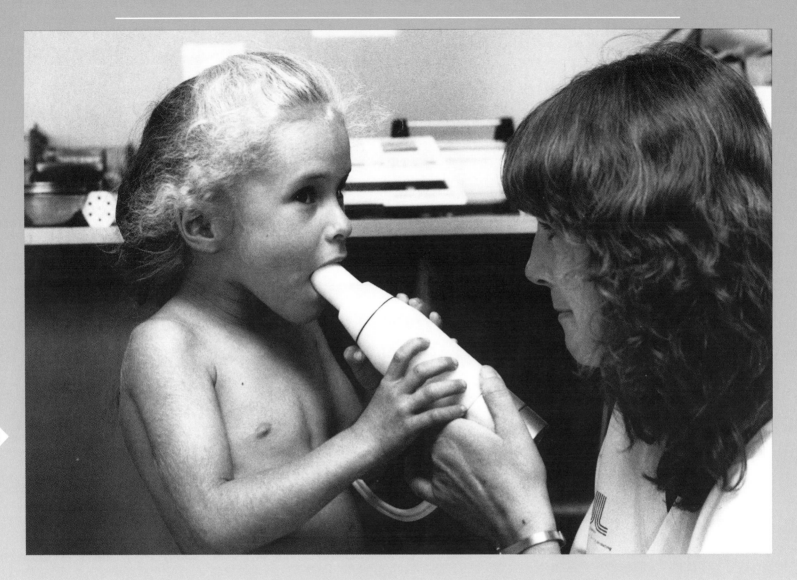

When Isabell arrives at the hospital, the nurse asks her to blow into a machine that will measure the speed of her exhalation. The machine is called a spirometer. Isabell blows into it a couple of times, and then the nurse notices that Isabell is breathing very hard. The nurse has Isabell use the inhaler that contains the medicine that widens bronchi, or airways. Isabell waits a little while and blows into the machine again. This time, it is much easier. With this test, called a pulmonary function test, the doctors can tell a lot about the condition of Isabell's bronchi. This will help them determine how much medicine she needs. The nurse also gives Isabell a skin test. She drips different substances on Isabell's forearm and then pricks Isabell's skin to allow the substances to get inside. If any of the spots become red or swollen, Isabell is allergic to that substance.

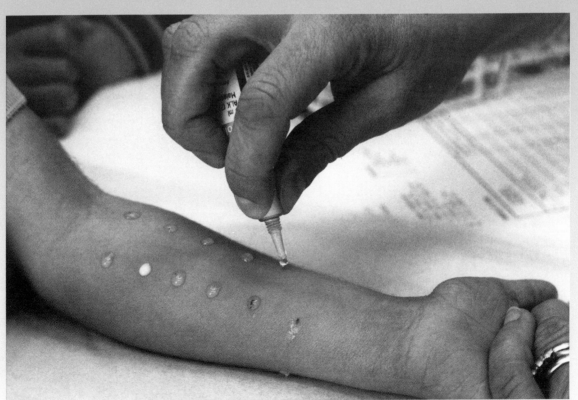

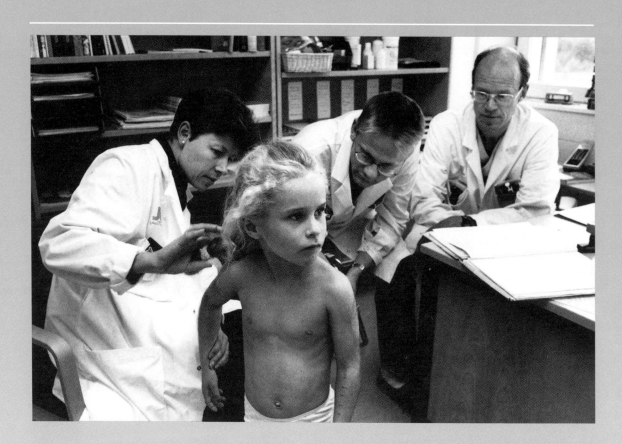

12

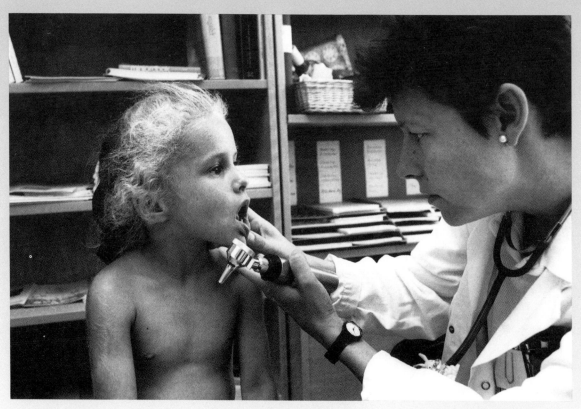

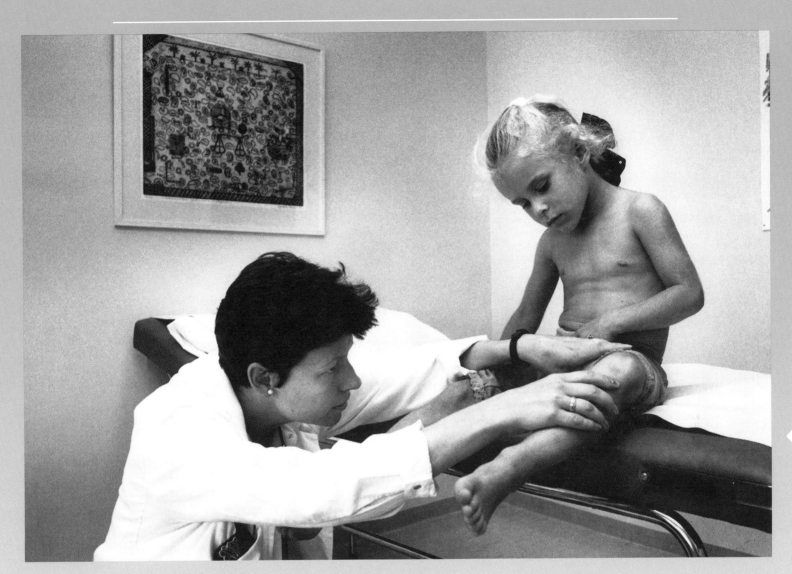

Finally, after all this testing, Isabell sees the doctor. Two other doctors from the dermatology clinic are with Isabell's doctor, Dr. Gunilla Hedlin, today. They examine Isabell carefully. They see that her skin is very dry, which causes it to itch and get infected easily. Isabell's mother tells the doctors that the medicine doesn't seem to help the itching. She asks if there is another medicine that might be better. Meanwhile, the doctors also examine the spots from the skin test. Several of the spots are already swollen. Dr. Gunilla asks Isabell about her asthma and wants to know if the asthma medicine is working. Isabell says that her asthma is not bothering her at the moment. But she tells the doctor that some days, when there is a lot of pollen in the air, she can't even go outside. Dr. Gunilla studies the results of the lung test. The report looks good.

Sometimes Isabell wishes she could have candy and ice cream like other children do. When she goes to the supermarket with her mother, Isabell eyes the shelves lined with candy and the big freezer full of ice cream. She thinks it is unfair that she can't sometimes have an ice cream cone when her friend Madelene has one. But Isabell knows that ice cream is made of several ingredients, such as milk proteins, to which she is allergic. Even a tiny taste could make her sick.

Unfortunately, ice cream isn't the only food that Isabell can't eat. She has never tasted a hamburger. An ordinary bun contains a kind of flour that would make her very sick, and all nuts are definitely out of the question. These foods, among others, such as yogurt, are very dangerous for her.

15

Horses, dogs, and other furry animals also cause Isabell serious trouble. Wherever there are animals, there are tiny particles of animal skin, hair, or feathers. These particles, known as dander, are spread easily – carried by the air or in dust, or stuck in clothes and hair. When such particles are present, Isabell's nose runs, her eyes itch, and her skin becomes very irritated. Worst of all, her breathing is affected. If she is not careful, she will have to go to the hospital.

Isabell's eczema makes her skin itch. She says that, at times, the itching almost drives her crazy. Her face, arms, and tummy itch. She scratches and scratches. At the day-care center where she goes to school, Isabell often asks the teacher to scratch her back.

Isabell is good about taking the medicine that is supposed to prevent itching, even though it makes her very tired. Changing clothes more frequently is also supposed to help stop the itching. So Isabell has a big trunk full of her different outfits at the day-care center. These clothes, as well as everything she wears, have to be made of pure cotton.

In spring and summer, Isabell sometimes gets very lonely. During these seasons, there are days when the air is filled with pollen, and she must stay indoors. She can't even visit her friends at their homes because when it is warm, most people open their windows. In her friends' homes, Isabell would have no protection from the pollen and dust.

Isabell's mother doesn't open windows even on warm days like this one. The family keeps only plastic flowers and some green plants in the house. Despite such precautions today, Isabell's nose is running, her eyes are itching, and she is having trouble breathing as she sits at the kitchen table looking outside. It is a lovely spring day, and the house is hot and sticky, but Isabell knows that the pollen outside would only make her feel worse.

Isabell longs for the days when she and her mother will be able to sleep late in the mornings. But for now, she continues to rise early and go through the morning routine of baths, salves, and medicines.

Today, Isabell and her mother are going to make a banana cake. Among other things, it contains water, bananas, and the kind of flour that does not make Isabell sick. Isabell pours the ingredients into the bowl and stirs them together. Soon the batter is ready to go into the oven.

While the cake bakes, Isabell's mother talks about
the time she gave Isabell cake that had eggs in it.
Isabell got very sick to her stomach and had
trouble breathing. Lotta feels badly about that
even now, but Isabell laughs and gives her mother
a big hug and a kiss. It isn't easy to remember all
the foods that she can't eat, Isabell insists.

By now, the banana cake is ready to eat. Isabell
takes a big piece and declares that it is delicious.

Isabell, Frederick, and their mother go on a two-week vacation to the sea. Isabell loves the summer! She can swim and go rowing in their little rowboat almost whenever she wants. She runs with Frederick to the pier where their mother is waiting. Isabell shouts that she wants to go rowing. Although it looks as if it might rain, both Isabell and her mother climb into the boat. Frederick stays on shore. He doesn't want to get caught in the rain.

Isabell takes hold of the oars and rows. She is quite good at rowing. The sun is still shining, but the sky is getting darker and darker. Some raindrops begin to fall. Isabell continues to row for a little while, but her arms are getting tired. She turns the boat and rows back to land again.

Isabell thinks she'd like to stay here all summer. She says the sea air makes her feel very strong. And besides, she could go rowing every day — even in the rain!

The vacation ends, and Isabell is back at her day-care center. Today, the children are going on a picnic. The teachers have decided to picnic at a little lake about half an hour's ride from the center. Everyone piles onto the bus, and the children sing merrily the whole way. At the lake, the children walk through the woods to their picnic area. When they catch sight of the lake, they start running. Soon everyone is in the water, and they all play and swim for a long time. After a while, Isabell gets out of the water, changes out of her swimsuit, and plays in the sand. The children have pancakes for lunch. Isabell's pancakes are a little different from the rest because they aren't made with eggs or ordinary flour, but Isabell likes them anyway. The cook always makes pleasant surprises. As Isabell eats, she sighs happily. A day at the beach always makes her feel so good.

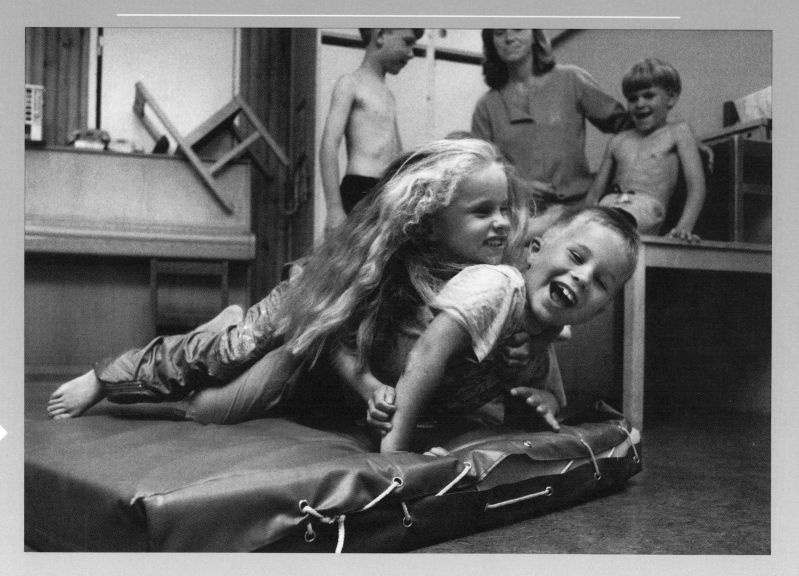

Back at the center, Isabell and some of the other children tumble playfully across the floor. Isabell is a tough little wrestler. She easily throws over her opponents. At home, Isabell often wrestles with Frederick. Although Frederick is strong, too, Isabell goes at him like a tiger. One of the teachers stands nearby watching the wrestling match. She observes that this struggle is a lot like Isabell's struggle with her allergies and asthma. In both struggles, Isabell is determined to win.

All the children run off to play in the garden. Isabell finds a little snail crawling up a tree. She says the snail is very sweet. She is not the least bit afraid of it. She touches the little animal gently, and she can touch it without getting ill.

Next autumn, Isabell and the other six-year-olds will start regular school. Every Tuesday before then, they are getting together to prepare themselves for the big day. This Tuesday, they are working with their senses. They start with the sense of taste. The sense of taste is very important to Isabell.

The teacher has put different vegetables in some cups. With their eyes closed, the children must taste, smell, and feel the vegetables. Mikaela begins, cautiously tasting, smelling, and feeling the first vegetable. It's disgusting, she shouts, but she cannot say what it is until everyone has had a turn. Isabell soon knows what the vegetable is, too, and she whispers the answer to her teacher. It's a tomato! Isabell must not eat that!

Next, the children play a game called Blind Man's Bluff. Elli begins. The children blindfold her and spin her around. She walks forward, stops, then touches the other children's faces. After just a few seconds, she discovers Isabell. It's easy to tell which one is Isabell, Elli states, because she always smells so nice, and her hair is so soft.

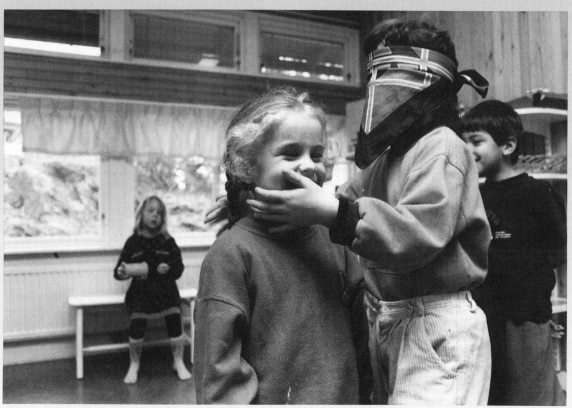

It's time for physical education in the gym of the regular school. The children laugh and shout happily as they enter the locker room to change their clothes. In the gym, they jump and dance excitedly as they wait for class to begin. Being in the regular school makes them feel like big kids. They enjoy exercising, and they get to use all the different equipment.

The teacher begins the class with some exercises. Then he tells the children to form a circle and close their eyes. He asks them to walk toward the center of the ring and take someone's hand. The children get themselves all mixed up. When they finally open their eyes, they just laugh.

Physical education is one of Isabell's favorite school activities. She likes the way it makes her feel and knows it is good for her. She wishes she could come to the gym every day — not just on Tuesdays.

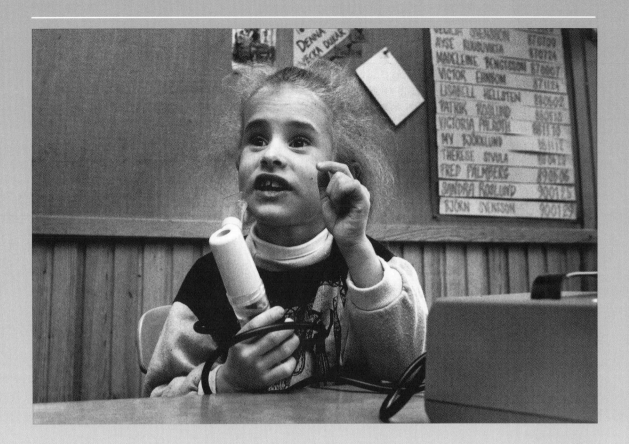

No matter where she is, Isabell's day always includes taking medicine. She has to use an inhaler called a nebulizer at the same time every day. It takes half an hour. Isabell does needlework while she waits. Before she knows it, the time is up, and she is breathing much better.

The children in the six-year-old group have gathered together again at an art studio. Each of them is making a little book about herself or himself. On the first page, Isabell has drawn a self-portrait. A picture of her family fills the second page. On the next page, she has drawn her hands. All of the children are also including their footprints in their books. To do this, they must have their feet painted. They take off their shoes and socks and wait for their turn.

Isabell delightedly watches the other children getting their feet painted. Now it is her turn. She is very ticklish and laughs the entire time the teacher paints her feet. She is eager to see how her footprint will look.

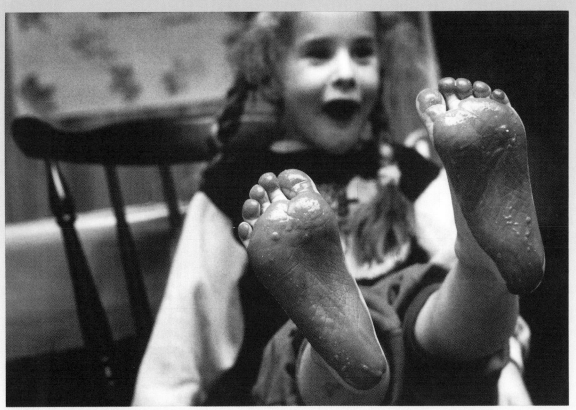

Having friends is important to children, and Isabell is no different. But when Isabell gets together with friends, she must often play with them out-of-doors. Other people's homes may have pets, carpets, or other dust-collecting items. Few homes are as free of irritants as Isabell's home.

Isabell almost always finds children on the playground. Today, as Isabell opens the park gate, Madelene greets her and asks if they can play on the swings together. Isabell loves the swings. Later, the girls join two boys on the seesaw. The boys seesaw very hard and fast. The girls must jump up as the seesaw hits the ground, or they will fly up off their seats. Isabell and Madelene spend most of the afternoon on the playground, chatting and laughing. Too soon, it is time to go home.

The next day, the children return to the art studio. Each of them has an easel with a real canvas. Isabell puts on a pinafore, takes some odorless paint, and begins painting. On the canvas, she paints a colorful sky, a house surrounded by big apple trees, and a lawn filled with lots of flowers. Far away on the horizon, she paints the sea. It makes Isabell think of her vacation at the sea this past summer. She loves the summer, even if it does cause her a lot of trouble. She hopes that as she gets older, her asthma and at least some of her allergies will disappear. Then, maybe, she will be able to eat ice cream.

Isabell's mother worries about the different situations that Isabell might face when she starts school in the autumn. Will the school make food that Isabell can eat? Will there be grown-ups to help Isabell take her medicine at the right time? Who will take care of her if she doesn't feel well? The teachers and other adults at school will have to handle these problems every day throughout the school year, just as Isabell must each day of her life.

QUESTIONS ABOUT ALLERGIES AND ASTHMA

Sometimes we can become confused or upset by people who are different from us. Getting the answers to questions is one way of gaining more understanding about people with allergies or asthma and lessening any confusion. Here are some of the most frequent questions that children and adults ask.

Can a person catch allergies or asthma?
No, you can't catch either allergies or asthma the way you can catch a cold or the flu. Since there are no viruses or bacteria at the root of either of these problems, allergies or asthma cannot be transferred between people.

The tendency toward allergic diseases, including both allergies and asthma, however, can be hereditary. That means that if these diseases run in your family, you have a greater chance of getting them than a friend who has no history of these problems in her or his family.

What is asthma?
Asthma is a common disease of the bronchi, or airways, leading to the lungs. Its name comes from Greek words meaning "to pant" or "breathe hard." As the name suggests, difficult breathing is a primary characteristic of asthma. In fact, the term "breathing difficulties" is probably one of the simplest ways to define this disease, and it covers a range of problems that asthma patients experience. At the root of these problems are overly sensitive bronchial tubes. In people with asthma, the bronchial tubes react more than necessary to certain stimuli, called triggers. For this reason, people with asthma are said to have "twitchy airways."

Asthma is a serious disease, but it is important to know that it is also reversible. This means that it does no permanent damage to either the lungs or airways. Treatment is aimed at preventing attacks. Either the body itself or medicines prescribed by a doctor will open the airways, reduce the mucus, and calm the coughing and wheezing. This reversibility factor sets asthma apart from many other respiratory diseases, such as emphysema. Emphysema does damage to both the lungs and the alveoli, or air sacs, within them. This damage is generally permanent.

How does a person know if he or she has asthma?
Symptoms that suggest asthma include a constant shortness of breath, wheezing, coughing, feelings of tightness in the chest, and an excessive amount of mucus in the airways and lungs. But as is true with any disease, symptoms can vary greatly from person to person. Some people who have asthma may experience only a soft cough without any wheezing or with wheezing that can only be heard with a doctor's stethoscope. Others may endure a serious shortness of breath or a wheezing that can be heard across the room. Most people's symptoms fall somewhere between these two examples.

A person with asthma will find that these symptoms tend to increase in particular situations: when visiting a friend who has a pet, at a change of the seasons, or after particularly strenuous exercise. But even this is not a sure-fire way to determine that particular ailments are caused by asthma. If you suspect that you have asthma, you should see a doctor. The doctor will study your family history and give you breathing tests similar to some of those that Isabell had. This type of information will help the doctor determine whether asthma is the problem.

What triggers an asthma attack?
While allergies such as those Isabell has are a leading trigger for asthma attacks, they are not the only cause. Other causes, or triggers, include:

• Exercise. Strenuous, continuous exercise has been

known to trigger asthma. For this reason, many people believe that asthma patients shouldn't exercise. But in reality, most people who have asthma can and should enjoy many types of exercise with the guidance of a doctor.

• Infection. Infections caused by either bacteria or viruses can bring on asthma attacks. Those caused by viruses, such as colds and flu, however, seem to be even more of a problem for asthma patients.

• Environmental conditions and irritants. This group of asthma triggers includes many, many items. Among them, just to name a few: dust, smog, and other pollutants; changes in the weather; smoke from cigars, cigarettes, or burning leaves; perfume, exhaust fumes, and other strong odors. All of these things and many more can cause an asthma attack.

• Drugs and food additives. Allergies to both drugs and food additives such as dyes and preservatives are often found at the root of an asthma attack. Aspirin and drugs containing aspirin are well-known triggers. Recent studies have shown that about one in five asthma patients are sensitive to aspirin. And food additives such as yellow dye #5 (Tartrazine) also lead to asthma attacks. This dye is found in many types of food, from candy, soft drinks, and dry cereals to puddings, cake mixes, and even medicine.

What happens during an asthma attack?
An asthma attack begins when a person's bronchial tubes and lung tissues react to the presence of one or more of the trigger factors – infections, irritating substances, allergies, etc. Then the asthmatic person's overly sensitive bronchial tubes and lung tissues begin to constrict. As muscles around the airways contract, the passageways themselves

narrow. This makes breathing difficult and cuts airflow to and from the lungs. Mucous membranes lining the airways begin to swell and produce even more mucus, which clogs already narrow air passageways. By this time, breathing often becomes so difficult that air passing in and out of the lungs becomes a whistlelike wheeze.

How common is asthma?
It is estimated that from 2 to 20 percent of people in the world's industrialized nations suffer from asthma. In the United States alone, that means more than ten million people struggle with this disease every day. Overall, 10 to 15 percent of children have had the disease at some time. In fact, among children, asthma is the leading cause for both hospitalization and time lost from school.

What about allergies? How common are they?
Some figures say that as many as half the people in the world have allergies or allergy-related diseases.

Can a person really outgrow asthma?
Yes, it is possible to "outgrow" asthma. Just as this disease can occur at any age, it can also disappear at any time. But because asthma is so unpredictable, a person who once had the disease is always in danger of having flare-ups. When asthma symptoms do improve or disappear, however, it is commonly among people who developed asthma as children. According to some figures, as many as three out of four children will be asthma-free by their early teens. Some doctors think that this improvement occurs as the child grows and her or his airways increase in size. Others suggest that the asthmatic child's body learns to protect itself. The answer is still unclear.

But for many other people, asthma remains a chronic condition with which they must learn to live.

Is there a pattern to asthma?

Where asthma continues to be a problem, it sometimes at least begins to follow a set pattern. This may seem small, but it can mean a lot to the person with asthma because recognizing any type of pattern will help control the disease. For example, if a person knows that spring allergies commonly bring on a heavy asthma season, she or he will know to be alert to any early signs of an oncoming attack at that time each year. She or he might even be able to be extra careful about avoiding allergens then. Through such preparation, more severe asthma attacks can be avoided.

What symptoms tell a doctor that someone has allergies?

Unfortunately, symptoms that are commonly linked to allergies are also symptoms of many other health problems. That sometimes makes it difficult for a doctor to determine an allergy or its source. But most patients who are diagnosed as having allergies usually list some combination of the following symptoms:

- A runny nose, watery eyes, and repeated sneezing.
- Wheezing or a shortness of breath. Although these symptoms may point to asthma, they can also be the result of allergies. Asthma and allergies are often closely linked.
- Skin problems such as rashes, hives, or other types of irritations.

- Diarrhea and nausea.
- Headaches and fatigue.

How do allergens get into our bodies?

Allergens make their way into the human body in any number of different ways. In fact, they get in using many of the same paths used by microorganisms (germs). One easy way for allergens to enter the body is through contact with our skin or mucous membranes. They can also get in as the result of insect stings. Commonly, however, allergens are breathed in or brought in through the foods we eat and the liquids we drink.

What is a scratch test?

A scratch test is a skin test that helps doctors determine what, if anything, a person is allergic to. In this test, the doctor introduces diluted amounts of common allergens (such as dust, animal dander, or pollen) to a patient's skin and watches for a reaction. Small drops of these substances are placed on a patient's skin — usually on the back or forearm. Then the doctor gently scratches each test area so that the patient's skin absorbs a small amount of the substance. Within about fifteen minutes, the doctor will check the tested areas for reactions. A common reaction is a raised area, called a wheal, surrounded by a reddish area, or flare. This most likely indicates an allergic reaction. The size of the inflamed area gives the doctor an idea of just how allergic the patient is to that particular substance.

44

THINGS TO DO AND THINK ABOUT

By doing these projects, you'll learn more about people living with allergies and asthma.

1. Imagine you suddenly develop allergies similar to Isabell's allergies. What types of changes might you have to make to your home environment? How might your allergies affect your school environment?

2. Isabell is allergic to many foods, including ice

cream and most sweets. Imagine being allergic to those foods. Think of and name all the situations in which you might find and be tempted to eat them.

3. Do you know someone who has allergies, asthma, or both? If so, talk to that person about what effect the condition has had on her or his life. What sort of medical routine does he or she follow? Does that routine include regular doses of medicines? Does your friend have to avoid certain situations or foods?

4. Investigate the human immune system. You'll find excellent explanations of this system in many books, including those on allergies, asthma, and human biology. Ask your teacher to discuss the immune system with your class.

5. Do a little research on allergies. From your reading, can you tell the difference between being sensitive to a particular substance and being allergic to it?

6. Does your city have an allergy or asthma group among its organizations? If so, find out if that organization provides speakers to local schools or clubs. Your teacher or club leader may be interested in having a speaker come to tell you more about allergies and asthma.

7. Certain food additives such as Tartrazine (yellow dye #5) seem to be especially common triggers for people with asthma. Check the ingredients on products in your home. Can you find examples of foods with that dye in them?

WHERE TO WRITE FOR MORE INFORMATION

The following organizations can give you more information about allergies and asthma. When you write to one of these organizations, be sure to include your name, address, and a stamped, self-addressed envelope for a reply.

Allergy/Asthma Information Association
65 Tromley Drive, Suite 10
Etobicoke, Ontario M9B 5Y7

American Academy of Allergy and Immunology
611 East Wells Street
Milwaukee, WI 53202

(Your local Lung Association or)
American Lung Association
1740 Broadway
New York, NY 10019-4374

The Asthma Foundation of New Zealand
P.O. Box 1459
Wellington, New Zealand

Allergy and Asthma Network
Mothers of Asthmatics, Inc.
3554 Chain Bridge Road, Suite 200
Fairfax, VA 22030

National Institute of Allergy and Infectious Diseases
National Institute of Health
Building 31, #7A50
9000 Rockville Pike
Bethesda, MD 20892

Australian Association of
   Asthma Foundations
P.O. Box 360
Woden Act 2606
Australia

MORE READING MATERIAL ABOUT ALLERGIES AND ASTHMA

The allergies and asthma publications listed below are about and for young people.

Allergies. Newman and Newman Layfield (Franklin Watts)

Allergies — What They Are, What They Do. Seixas (Greenwillow)

Asthma: The Complete Guide to Self-Management of Asthma and Allergies for Patients and Their Families. Weinstein (McGraw-Hill)

Children with Asthma. Plaut (Pedipress)

Hometown Hero. Aiello (Twenty-First Century Books)

I'm a Meter Reader. Sander (Allen & Hanburys)

The publications listed below provide in-depth information about allergies and asthma.

All About Asthma. Paul and Fafoglia (Sterling)

Allergies: The Complete Guide to Diagnosis, Treatment, and Daily Management. Young, Dobozin, Miner (Consumer Report Books)

The Allergy Self-Help Book. Faelten and editors of *Prevention* magazine (Rodale)

Essential Asthma Book: A Manual for Asthmatics of All Ages. Haas and Sperber Haas (Scribner's Sons)

The Whole Way to Allergy Relief Prevention: A Doctor's Complete Guide to Treatment & Self-Care. Krohn (Hartley & Marks)

Newsletters containing up-to-date information on allergies and asthma are listed below.

AAIA Quarterly. Allergy/Asthma Information Association, 65 Tromley Drive, Etobicoke, Ontario M9B 5Y7. (This quarterly publication contains updates on allergy/asthma treatment.)

Allergy News. Suite 150, 27800 Medical Center Road, Mission Viejo, CA 92691. (This newsletter is written by two doctors and is available free.)

The Asthma and Allergy Advocate. American Academy of Allergy and Immunology, 611 East Wells Street, Milwaukee, WI 53202. (This quarterly publication contains practical information and health tips from allergists.)

Asthma Update. 123 Monticello Avenue, Annapolis, MD 21401. (This asthma-related newsletter reviews medical literature for new information about asthma.)

MA Report. Mothers of Asthmatics, Inc., 3554 Chain Bridge Road, Suite 200, Fairfax, VA 22030. (This newsletter provides information for parents of children with asthma.)

GLOSSARY OF WORDS ABOUT ALLERGIES AND ASTHMA

allergen: a foreign substance that causes an allergic reaction within the body. Common allergens include pollens, molds, animal dander, foods, or chemicals in the water, air, and food.

allergic reaction: the symptoms or group of symptoms that result when the body is exposed to allergens.

allergy: a condition in which the body has an overly sensitive reaction to certain substances. In such situations, the body's immune system attacks harmless or even useful substances that the body identifies as foreign.

antibody: a protein molecule produced by the body's immune system in response to substances that the body perceives as foreign or abnormal. As part of the immune system, antibodies protect the body from these substances by attacking and destroying them.

antigen: any substance that, upon entering the body, is perceived as foreign by that body's immune system and thus causes the production of antibodies.

asthma: a common lung disease in which there is reversible obstruction of the bronchial tubes, or airways. This obstruction, which can be caused by a narrowing of the airways, or an increase in the production of mucus, or both, is often the result of an allergic reaction. An asthma attack can be eased by the body itself or with the help of medicines.

bronchi: either of the two large airways that lead into the right and left lungs.

bronchioles: the smaller airways that branch off of the bronchi and lead to the tiny alveoli or air sacs.

chronic: always present; constant.

constrict: to squeeze or draw together; to tighten around an object so as to inhibit movement.

dander: small particles of animal hair, skin, or feathers. Dander is not visible to the naked eye.

eczema: a dry, itchy skin condition often caused by or connected with food allergies. In children, milk is often the cause of an eczema problem, although many other foods can trigger it.

immune system: the means by which the body protects itself from what it perceives as infection. This system includes specialized cells, organs, and body fluids.

mucous membrane: the lining of body passages and cavities, such as the mouth, throat, and nose, that makes a connection with the outside world.

mucus: a sticky body fluid that coats, moistens, and protects the membranes that produce it.

pulmonary function test: a test that measures how well a person's lungs work. The test determines how much air the lungs can hold (capacity) and how quickly the lungs can move the air (function).

spirometer: the instrument used in a pulmonary function test to measure the amount and speed of the air moving in and out of the lungs.

symptom: a change in a person's physical or mental condition that indicates the presence of a disease, disability, or other medical condition.

INDEX